D0850276

Scary Creatures
HIPPOS

DISCARD

Forbush Memorial Library
PO Box 468
118 Main Street
Westminster MA 01473

Written by
Penny Clarke

Franklin Watts®
An Imprint of Scholastic Inc.
NEW YORK • TORONTO • LONDON • AUCKLAND • SYDNEY
MEXICO CITY • NEW DELHI • HONG KONG
DANBURY, CONNECTICUT

Created and designed
by David Salariya

Author:

Penny Clarke is an author and editor specializing in nonfiction books for children. She has written books on natural history, rain forests, and volcanoes, as well as others on different periods of history. She used to live in central London, but thanks to modern technology she has now fulfilled her dream of being able to live and work in the countryside.

Artists:

Janet Baker & Julian
  Baker (JB Illustrations)
John Francis
Li Sidong
Robert Morton

Series Creator:

David Salariya was born in Dundee, Scotland. In 1989 he established The Salariya Book Company. He has illustrated a wide range of books and has created many new series for publishers in the UK and overseas. He lives in Brighton, England, with his wife, illustrator Shirley Willis, and their son.

Editor: Tanya Kant

Editorial Assistant:
Rob Walker

Picture Research:
Mark Bergin

Photo Credits:
Dreamstime: 15
iStockphoto: 14, 17, 28
Jonathan Salariya: 4, 5, 8, 9, 13, 16, 25, 26, 27

Pygmy hippo

© The Salariya Book Company Ltd MMIX
All rights reserved. No part of this book may be reproduced, stored in a retrieval system, or transmitted in any form or by any means, electronic, mechanical, photocopying, recording, or otherwise, without the written permission of the copyright owner.

Created, designed, and produced by
The Salariya Book Company Ltd
25 Marlborough Place, Brighton BN1 1UB

A CIP catalog record for this title is available from the Library of Congress.

ISBN-13: 978-0-531-21671-2 (lib. bdg.)
978-0-531-21042-0 (pbk.)
ISBN-10: 0-531-21671-3 (lib. bdg.)
0-531-21042-1 (pbk.)

Published in 2010 in the United States by
Franklin Watts
An Imprint of Scholastic Inc.
557 Broadway
New York, NY 10012

Printed in China

PAPER FROM
SUSTAINABLE
FORESTS

Contents

Common hippo

What Are Hippos?

Hippopotamuses, also called hippos, are large **mammals**. Their name, which means "river horse" in Greek, gives a clue about their lives. They spend most of their time swimming in African rivers and lakes or grazing along their banks.

Did You Know?

Hippos are good swimmers. They have webbed toes that help them paddle through the water. When they dive, they can close their nostrils so they don't breathe in water.

Hippos spend most of the day like this—partly **submerged** in water. They come on land to feed and sun themselves on the riverbank.

Did You Know?

Adult male hippos weigh up to 4 tons. They are nearly 16 feet (5 m) long and 5 feet (1.5 m) tall at the shoulder. Females are slightly smaller and lighter.

Why Are Hippos Scary?

Hippos are large and aggressive—that's why they're scary!
They will attack anyone, human or wild animal, who comes near
their **territory**. The hippo in the photo above is not yawning.
Opening its mouth like this to show its teeth is a warning—and
a threat.

Where Do Hippos Live?

Today there are two **species** of hippo—the pygmy hippo and the common hippo. Both live in rivers and lakes in Africa, south of the Sahara Desert. But **fossils** found by **paleontologists** show that hippos once lived in other parts of Africa, Asia, and Europe.

Today, pygmy hippos live in just a few parts of West Africa, from Guinea to Nigeria. Common hippos are more widespread. They live in east, central, and western Africa, from the edge of the Sahara Desert in the north to South Africa in the south.

Common hippo's foot

Did You Know?

Hippos have four toes on each foot. You can see them on the feet of the hippo on the table-of-contents page.

Seen from underneath, the four toes on the foot of a hippo are very obvious. Each toe has a protective nail. As a hippo walks, its feet spread to keep it from sinking into muddy riverbanks.

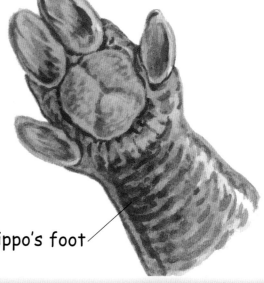

Pygmy hippo's foot

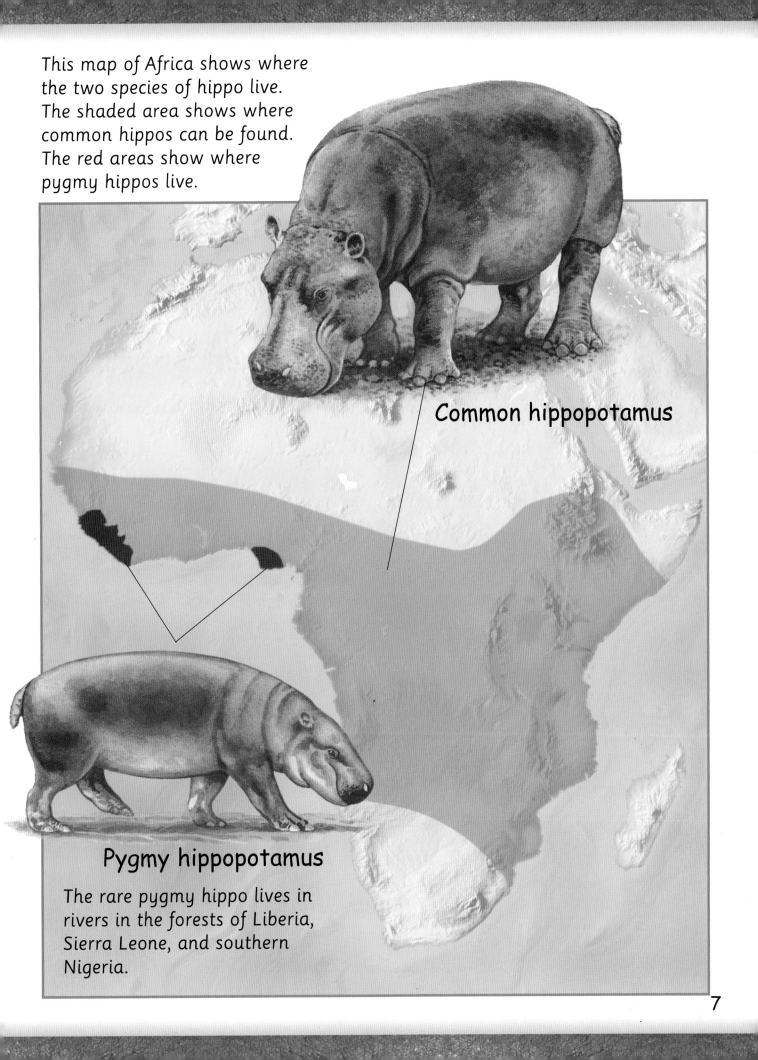

This map of Africa shows where the two species of hippo live. The shaded area shows where common hippos can be found. The red areas show where pygmy hippos live.

Common hippopotamus

Pygmy hippopotamus

The rare pygmy hippo lives in rivers in the forests of Liberia, Sierra Leone, and southern Nigeria.

How Do Hippos Live?

Common hippos live in large, well-organized family groups. The oldest female leads the group. There is usually only one adult male in a group—when young males become adults, they must leave. If they don't leave on their own, the females will chase them out.

Each hippo group has its own **crèche**—an area where mother hippos take care of each others' young. The crèche is usually on the bank of a river or lake or on a sandbar in the middle of a river. The females and young gather at the crèche when they are not feeding or in the water.

These two young hippos are getting ready to fight. Adult males use their huge tusks to fight over territory, mates, and feeding grounds.

Did You Know?

Fighting hippos may break each other's legs. A broken leg means death because the victim will no longer be able to stand, swim, or walk.

A crèche of young hippos gathers by the bank of the Mara River in Kenya.

How Do Hippos Feed?

Hippos are **herbivores**—they eat only plants. Because they are such big animals, they need to eat huge amounts of plant material. Each evening, hippos leave the water and walk to where they will feed that night.

Male hippos are more **solitary** than females and go alone to the feeding grounds. Each male has his own path and marks it with dung to warn others off.

Although hippos are bigger than cattle, they eat less food. That's because hippos don't need much energy to move about in the water.

X-Ray Vision

Hold the next page up to the light and see what's inside a hippo.

See What's Inside

Female hippos feeding on the riverbank

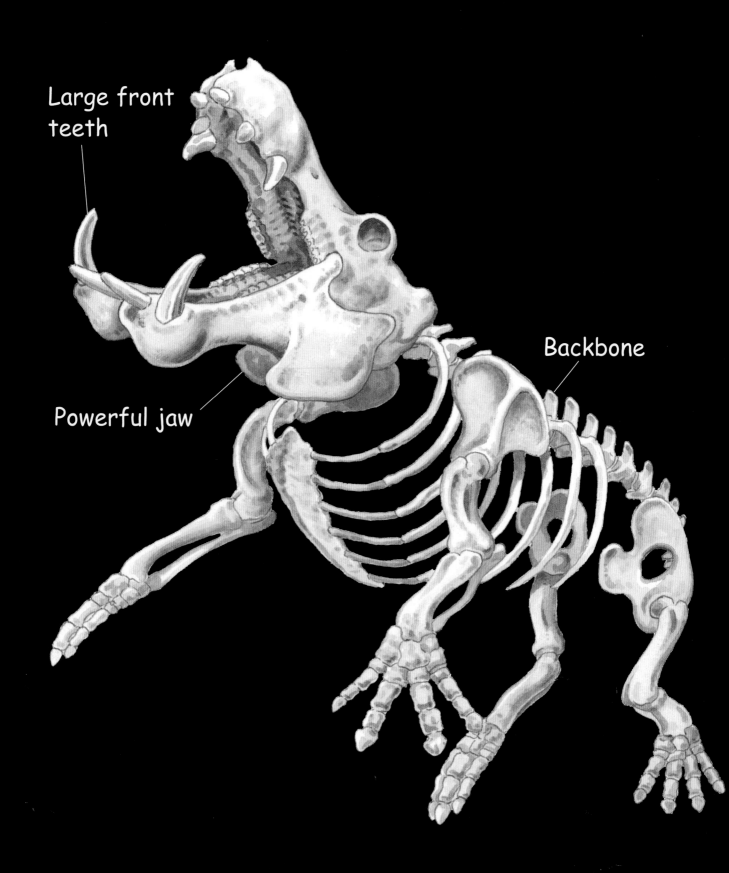

Large front teeth

Powerful jaw

Backbone

Do Hippos Have Enough Food?

Plants grow fast in the warm **habitats** where hippos live, so most of the time, there is plenty of food. Female hippos usually have their babies early in the wet season, when the heavy rainfall makes the grass grow faster.

Did You Know?

Hippos eat grass and other plants but will also eat fruit that has fallen from trees growing along the riverbank.

Hippo grazing on the riverbank

Are All Hippos Huge?

No! Compared to the common hippo, pygmy hippos are very small. Adults are only about 6 feet (1.9 m) long and 2.6 feet (0.8 m) tall at the shoulder. Because pygmy hippos are smaller, they are also much lighter. They weigh a quarter of a ton; a common hippo weighs 3 to 4 tons.

Pygmy hippos live by streams flowing through the dense forests of West Africa. They rarely come into the open. Their diet includes grasses, **tubers**, fallen fruit, and aquatic plants.

A pygmy hippo swims through floating plants in an African stream.

Did You Know?

Pygmy hippos spend less time in water than common hippos, and only the toes on their front feet are webbed.

A pygmy hippo bares its teeth as a warning to an intruder—probably the photographer. They look fierce, but pygmy hippos are shy creatures that prefer to run from danger, rather than stand and fight.

Are Hippos Bald?

A hippo isn't completely bald, even though it may look hairless in photos like the one below. The hairiest part of a hippo is the end of its tail. It also has hair on its chin, **muzzle**, and ears. If you could stroke a hippo's chin, the hair would feel like stiff bristles.

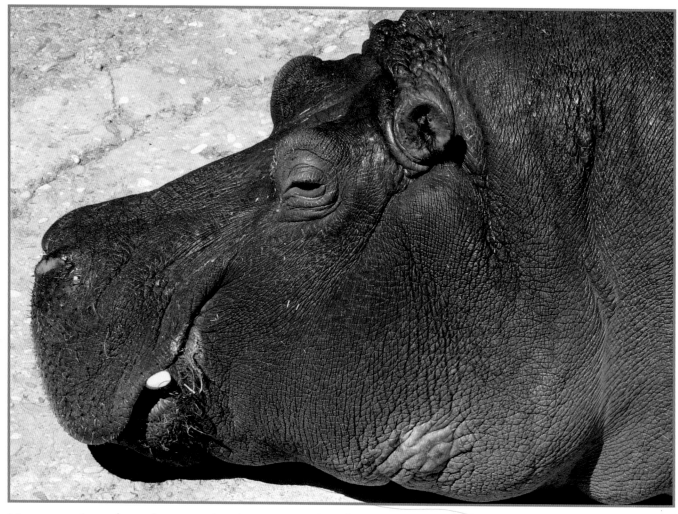

You can just barely see the hairs on this hippo's muzzle.

Were hippos once hairy? Did they lose their hair after spending so many generations in the water? No one knows. Although hippos don't have hair to protect their skin, they do release a protective substance called "pink sweat."

Hairy muzzle

Hairy ears

Hairy chin

Did You Know?

Scientists classify hippos as **artiodactyls**: herbivores with an even number of hoof-like toes. Pigs, camels, sheep, and cattle are also artiodactyls.

Sometimes hippos look as if they have shiny skin. They don't. Their skin is rather dull; it's the pink sweat that makes their skin shine.

Pink sweat protects hippos' skin from long periods in water. It is a pink, oily substance that hippos **secrete** from special **glands** in the fatty layer under their skin.

Pink sweat

Were There Ancient Hippos?

Paleontologists have found hippo fossils in northwestern Europe that are about 120,000 years old. These ancient hippos looked much like the hippos living today, except that their eyes were very high on their heads.

Europe 120,000 years ago

Straight-tusked elephants

Fossils can tell us what Earth was like in the past, what plants and animals there were, and what the climate was like.

Ancient rhino

Raised eye

Ancient hippos

Raised eyes helped ancient hippos to see clearly above the water when they swam.

Did You Know?

Hippo hunting was a favorite sport of the **pharaohs** (ancient Egyptian kings).

Today, hippos don't live in the part of the Nile River that flows through Egypt, but **archeologists** think they once did. The ancient Egyptians painted hippos on the walls of their tombs and made thousands of models of them. These little hippos pictured below are copies of ornaments that date from about 2000 B.C. The flowers painted on their backs represent the abundance of life in and around the Nile.

Clay model

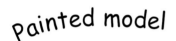

Painted model

Hippos were a dangerous nuisance to the ancient Egyptians. Each year hippos killed hundreds of people, attacking and capsizing (overturning) their small boats. Hippos also ate the crops growing in the fields beside the Nile.

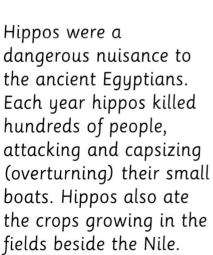

Copy of a wall painting

19

God or Monster?

Long ago, many people believed that gods visited Earth in the shape of powerful animals. The ancient Egyptians were no exception. Because hippos are powerful, dangerous animals, ancient Egyptians believed Seth, their god of evil, was a hippo.

Ancient Egyptian gods, such as Seth the hippo, were usually painted as humans with the heads of wild animals.

Good or Evil?

Egyptians didn't always consider hippos evil. Taweret, the goddess who helped women when they were giving birth, was part hippo.

Ancient Egyptian god Seth

X-Ray Vision

Hold the next page up to the light to see what happens when a hippo meets an ancient Egyptian boat.

See What Happens

Reed fishing boat

Hunting hippos was exciting but very dangerous. Men armed with stone-tipped spears hunted hippos from fragile reed boats.

What Was an Ancient Egyptian Hippo Hunt Like?

Ancient Egyptian wall paintings show us what hippo hunts were like. Hunters would find hippos in the waters and reed-filled marshes of the Nile and hunt them from small boats made of **papyrus** reeds.

The ancient Egyptians believed their pharaoh was like a god. When he killed a hippo, he was protecting his people by striking a blow against the evil god Seth.

Ancient Egyptian drawing of a hippo hunt

Do Hippos Have Enemies?

Hippos are so large and aggressive that most animals will not risk attacking them. Occasionally a lion is seen leaping onto a hippo's back and slashing at its sides with its claws. But hippos have such tough skin that this usually does little damage. In fact, humans armed with weapons are the only enemies of hippos.

Despite weighing up to 4 tons, adult hippos run extremely fast—about 30 miles (48 km) per hour. If people get too near to their young, hippos will charge the intruders, trampling them if they fall.

Hippos will charge at anyone who comes too close.

The Egyptians and other ancient African peoples killed hippos with stone- and metal-tipped weapons.

Hippos gather in tight groups for safety.

Canine tooth

Did You Know?

Adult hippos' canine teeth are almost 3.3 feet (1 m) long. In some old males, they reach 5.6 feet (1.7 m)! (These measurements include the long roots needed to anchor such huge teeth in the jaw.)

Some people collect the ivory **canine teeth** of hippos and carve them into ornaments. This puts hippos at risk of being killed just for their teeth. Is making an ornament a good reason to kill an animal?

Are Hippos in Danger?

Female hippo with her young baby swimming beside her

The greatest dangers facing hippos (apart from being hunted) are climate change and habitat loss. Africa has two seasons: wet and dry. By the end of the dry season, the rivers and waterholes have shrunk and many species must compete for the little remaining water. In some areas, the dry season is getting longer and less rain is falling.

The destruction of forest habitats is a serious threat to pygmy hippos because they spend more time on land than common hippos. They also hide in vegetation when threatened or frightened.

Did You Know?

Baby hippos stay with their mothers for several years. When hippos look for food, the mother leads the way, and her babies follow one behind the other, the oldest last.

Can Mothers Hurt Their Babies?

The biggest threat facing a baby hippo can be its own mother. Hippos can move fast but are quite clumsy. Several tons of hippo charging into or out of the water could easily knock a baby over. Or the baby could be stepped on and crushed. Perhaps this is what happened to the young hippo below. But its death is not a waste, because its body provides food for other creatures.

Crocodile and monitor lizard approaching a dead baby hippo

Are Hippos Important?

Hippos are very important. They eat huge amounts of vegetation, keeping the banks clear for other creatures to reach the water. Because they eat so much, they produce enormous amounts of waste. This natural fertilizer helps sustain the **ecosystems** of the rivers and lakes where hippos live.

Did You Know?

The tons of waste an adult hippo excretes each year help plants, insects, and tiny water creatures to grow.

Sunlight shining through water dapples a submerged hippo's back.

Do Hippos Help Other Animals?

If hippos didn't eat waterside plants, some of the smaller creatures shown below would struggle to reach the water to drink. And rivers and lakes are sources of food as well as water. Tiny **invertebrates** that thrive on hippo dung are food for fish and insects. Then these animals are eaten by larger creatures—and so on up the **food chain**.

Did You Know?

In some areas, hippos eat all of the tall grass that lines the riverbank. This makes hunting difficult for **predators**, such as lions, because they need this grass to hide in as they stalk antelopes and other **prey**.

African pygmy goose

African fish eagle

Sitatunga

Common hippo

Otters

Dragonfly

Hippo Facts

The ancient Egyptians believed that one of the constellations (groups of stars visible in the night sky) was a hippo.

Adult hippos can stay underwater for more than five minutes.

Careless use of poisons endangers many animals. In Kenya, hippos have eaten plants treated with insecticides —chemicals used to kill insects that eat crops. These insecticides poisoned the hippos and then the animals that fed on their carcasses (dead bodies), including lions, hyenas, and vultures.

Female common hippos give birth every 18 months to two years. The babies are born about 34 weeks after mating. Pygmy hippos give birth after about 28 weeks.

Tourism is one of Africa's most important industries. Every year, thousands of visitors go to game parks to watch wildlife such as elephants, rhinos, hippos, and giraffes.

Hippos usually have just one baby at a time. Only very rarely do they have twins.

If a male hippo comes into a crèche or shows signs of aggression near young hippos, the adult females will attack him.

In areas where pygmy hippos have been hunted, they tend to hide in waterside vegetation and rarely come into the open.

Each group of hippos is very well organized. The babies stay near their mothers or another adult female. As they grow, the young hippos play with others of the same age and gender. The males practice fighting, and the females chase each other and roll around in the water.

Male hippos use dung to mark their territory. They flick their dung through the air by swishing their tails quickly from side to side, so that the dung covers as large an area as possible.

Glossary

archeologist Someone who studies the remains of past civilizations.

artiodactyl A mammal that has an even number of toes on each foot, but walks only on the third and fourth toes. These toes usually end in hooves or nails.

canine tooth A pointed tooth for tearing food.

crèche A group of young animals guarded by one or more adults.

ecosystem A group of organisms that depend on each other and their surroundings to survive.

food chain An arrangement of animals and plants in which each feeds on the one below it in the chain.

fossil The remains left by a plant or animal that lived long ago.

gland A body organ that produces a special substance.

habitat Wherever a plant or animal lives naturally.

herbivore An animal that eats only plants.

invertebrate An animal that has no backbone, such as a snail or worm.

mammal An animal that is born alive and then fed by its mother's milk.

muzzle The mouth, nose, and jaw parts of some animals.

paleontologist Someone who studies fossils and other ancient life-forms.

papyrus A type of reed used by the ancient Egyptians to make boats and paper.

pharaoh The title of the rulers of ancient Egypt.

predator An animal that hunts and kills other animals for food.

prey An animal hunted and eaten by a predator.

secrete To produce and give off a substance, such as sweat.

solitary Living alone.

species A group of animals or plants that look alike, live in the same way, and produce young that do the same.

submerged Covered by the water's surface.

territory A piece of land that a person or wild animal defends against intruders.

tuber A thick underground stem or root of a plant.

Index